Ossabaw

DAVID HAMILTON edits *The Iowa Review* and teaches English literature at the University of Iowa. With degrees from Amherst College (AB) and the University of Virginia (PhD), he taught in Colombia and at the University of Michigan before taking his present position. The University of Missouri Press published his *Deep River* (2001), a memoir embedded in local history reaching far into the archaeological record. In 1992, he was a Fulbright Professor in Valencia, Spain.

Ossabaw

David Hamilton

S
SALT

CAMBRIDGE

PUBLISHED BY SALT PUBLISHING
PO Box 937, Great Wilbraham, Cambridge PDO CB1 5JX United Kingdom

© David Hamilton, 2006

The right of David Hamilton to be identified as the
author of this work has been asserted by him in accordance
with Section 77 of the Copyright, Designs and Patents Act 1988.

First published 2006

Printed and bound in the United Kingdom by Lightning Source

Typeset in Swift 9.5 / 13

ISBN-13 978 1 84771 260 1 paperback
ISBN-10 1 84771 260 5 paperback

SP

1 3 5 7 9 8 6 4 2

for Rebecca

Contents

Acknowledgments

The following poems, often in varying form, appeared as follows: "On Never Ending with," *The American Scholar*; "Charlie Asked," *The American Voice*; "For Coyote, Song and Lament," "The Edge Is What I Have," and "On the Last Days of Fast Time," *Appearances*; "Oriole," "Papaver," and "Blinded," *Connecticut Review*; "Before the Jugs in Soaked Burlap, Before the Water," *Country Journal*; "After Claes Oldenburg," *Ekphrasis*; "Homage to Alfred Montgomery" and "His Armory Show, Nights of 1958" *Fulcrum*; "Flagging for Alfatox in a Middle Field," *The Harvard Magazine*; "The Blue He Seized," *The Hollins Critic*; "Kindnesses," *Michigan Quarterly Review*; "Many Moons," "For Rebecca," and "Poison, a partially found poem," *100 Words*; "Fable," *Poetry Northwest*; "Slender Batons" II and "The Ballad of Bender Sutton," *Quarterly West*; "Lovesong from the Marshes, " Festival," and "Serranilla of Aranjuéz," *River Oak Review*; "Book by Leaf," "Our Oldest Oath," "Neither Venice Nor Belmont," *Salt Flats Annual;* "Postcards," *Salt/Verse online*; "Gaudy Fox," *Seneca Review*; "Noctua" and "The Collector," *Southern Humanities Review*; "Slender Batons," I, III, and IV *Verse* and *Jacket*. "Poem Ending with Lines from an Obscure Memoir," "To a Later Autumn," "Haiku Composed During a Lecture," "Van Gogh Dropped," and eleven other poems listed above made up *The Least Hinge*, a Frith Press chapbook, 2002.

Lovesong from the Marshes

Think of grasses bending as the stream bends
Leaning against its sweep in from the margins
Holding on somewhere under as the tide gathers

Rising and falling to the wings of the heron
Pulling his old blue pleasure from one rill to another
   Over grasses bending as the stream bends
   Leaning against its sweep in from the margins

Where minnows worry a warp that softens
And the heron pulls his old blue pleasure
Over the long salty winding together
   Of grasses bending as the stream bends
   Leaning against its sweep in on a margin
   Holding on somewhere under as the tide gathers

For Rebecca

As we were becoming wing and wind, you
were also watching wildflowers. I'd
roam ahead on our walks, seeking quickness
in under brush or open sky while you
bent close to prairie smoke or pussy toes —
grayish cotton swabs foaming from a stem
so short that I had overlooked them. I
may always think of you bending to look
small flowers over and to save a leaf
within the pages of the guide you carried.
You found the hidden pod of the bloodroot
and watched until you could scatter its seed
as our seraphic, six-winged garden soared.

To a Later Autumn

In the distance like the wings of an egret
or a sheet shaken out falling over a bed
a bleached bank of shells lifts southward

a low Indian mound on the marsh
with an edge of wind-twisted cedars
some green some gray and weathered

barely vantage for lichen
but enough under the vulture
his smooth shadow passing

for sun in November
extravagant sun no matter how thin
on a trace of whomever was lugged

to this sad pile of silt cedar and oysters
where sifting salt water fills and then falls
away from his long sloughing to bone.

It won't do to make much of impermanence
neither ours nor the marshes'
which though vast die from our venturing on them.

All that is given
as we rush along dragging much with us.
How much will bleach out like these oysters

shucked and dropped over an eater?
Rushes stiffening still stand up to the vulture—
green brown and bronze—

a few golden shafts check his shadow
stretching for one
touch more of the sun of November.

"Go, Little Book"

Someone came along the way, wraithlike, leaning,
his gray, relic laughter clipping the land,
and hard, like silver: "Where is my lissome daughter,
her wheatleaf folded in this ancient ground?"
We heard his bitter meadowwalk,
his burnt oath, celestial, stir the dry nymph's tavern,
his pulsing shadow kicking up the sand.

Poem Ending with Lines from an Obscure Memoir

They took away his passport but not permission to travel.
He was twenty-five and had found authority
among men. One winter north of the Pripet Marshes
would measure the rest of his life. But first Moscow
before finding his long way home. The line at Lenin's
tomb was too long to bother. John Reed's grave
lay close by, untended, within the Kremlin wall.
He visited Tolstoy's home and learned of a grandson, Ilya,
younger than he and Quaker aided, who had herded
fifteen hundred head of horses across the steppes,
from Turkestan to Samara. He must have been well armed.
An English woman described corpses stacked like cordwood
then buried shallow as survivors hoarded their strength.
Men had eaten wolves and wolves had eaten men,
which explained one more rifle in Quaker hands.
He noted scratch marks where people had scraped fresh
dirt up over the graves. Riding third class, he granted
the practicality of roof riders' passing down the corpses
at the stations. The secret service agent, minding him,
asked about emigrating to America. Would there be
good land to farm? At Buzuluk, on the Samara River,
he watched the setting sun back light a pock-marked
courtyard wall. Admiral Kolchak and General Denikin
had been through, names soon muffled under the creak
of saddle leather and the slow thud of horses' hooves
in a snowy and distant Russian forest, with often a crow's
wings, folding and unfolding, that least hinge his horizon.

Gaudy Fox

I didn't do the owl any good,
Or the brown thrasher either, in his wood

Of one small tree, a cedar, seeking shelter
As I was passing, walking Ramón, and caught
His eye, enough to hint he was, he ought
To realize, quite closely looked after

For reasons he might not entirely admire.
So off he flew, across the street, like owl
From way up in the spruces while crows "crow-eled"
Unceasingly around him, their guns for hire.

Our trespassing—my willful seeing—focused
One pair of eyes too many and off he too,
Then, unlike fox, in repose by our path, the dew
Lavished on fur the flies had just noticed.

Our Oldest Oath

A hummingbird has chased away a bee.
She hardly missed a beat, made it look easy.

She was a she; she had no ruby throat.
I almost said "because," because she lacked,
She was. With white-tipped tail, wings wide, she tacked
On fragrant air. Nor did she misquote

Expressive hostas loud in their half circle
With nectar she'd defended from the bee.
That was the day that summer ended, carefree
As the air turned cool, an oracle

Of autumn, its lightest touch. I dug up
Clematis and a rose, transplanted both.
I could have bet she kept our oldest oath,
To keep on probing whatever's most corrupt.

Not at All Byzantine

Can you believe I spent four years polishing
their balls? Every day, in the equipment
room, where high on the wall, between the top shelf
and ceiling, plaster had been chipped away
around a pipe into the girls' locker room,
and where, if you wedged half of yourself
onto that shelf and left one foot dangling
toward the ladder, you might win peeks
at lots of very white underwear,
but where, routinely, I tumbled eighteen,
twenty or it usually seemed forty
basketballs out of a sack, squirted
sucky pink cleaning fluid
on each and wiped each off with a towel
so the balls were ready for practice
and our boys for the game before which
and at half times I ran a push broom over
the floor, working across center court from one
out-of-bounds line to the other. I packed
the trunks, handed uniforms out, took them back
sweaty, and loaded it all on the bus.
Once I locked the keys in a trunk, and the A-team
wore the wet rags of B-teamers after their game.

So passed four years as basketball manager,
sitting the bench, home and away, writing
the number of each player on a chart,
for each shot, and circling his number
if he made it. Reloading that trunk, riding
the bus with the team, and getting my dollar
peeled off a wad Coach pulled from a front pocket
of his pleated slacks, one buck for a burger,
shake, fries, and very small change, at the drive-in
as we returned to town, where cheerleaders waited,
and I'd squeeze into a booth with one or more girls
and an equal number of players, all
of which proved an apt limousine, set on cruise
for my career with a small magazine.

"The Edge Is What I Have"

after Roethke

Day by day, the eye begins to clear.
I find the owl that thickens
a jack pine's inner bough.

Swallows don't just vanish
but more deeply disappear,
downwind, along a stream,
releasing its last yellow.

> Then the heron sees me and veers
> upstream, patrolling his marshes,
> he won't accept me on them.

An eastwind's unhurried pushing
tilts the vulture's wing.
A harrier banks slowly,
teasing prey out of the marsh.

Within vastness, butterflies
pair off wing to wing,
while in the middle distance,
cord rolls from juncus grass.

> But the heron sees me and veers
> away, neither of us free
> in the searching wind.

Festival

Off, off goes the gulf fritillary, that phosphorous
backed butterfly, flaming out and out

over salt marshes. Like sparks blown into night
from dry grasses heaped on an open fire

only to throb a few quick beats into the dark,
so the fritillary touches its orange flutter

to the spartina marshes and kindles nothing.
The great, broad cloths of egrets, settling, would seem

to smother them. Even though they sometimes land
on dry palmetto fronds and hold their open flames

to those plausible torches, there is only
another slight heave, then more subsiding,

like the thought of an old love in a garden,
napping, and garlanded with fritillaries.

After Laʒamon

A Laʒamon lived among the people   a layman descended
from Camile and Leonard, Anna   and George, Leoné
and Theodor, in the Middle West   with its meadows and streams
its pretty good schools.   It could be serene
along meandering rivers   where he read and read
where it entered his mind   overwhelmed his thinking
how he reveled in   the ripe deeds of forebears
the bookish ones   even from England and before.
So Laʒamon went strolling   through second hand stores
and library stacks   lingering among his finds.
He carried to his carrel   American books and English
Chaucer, even a few   ancients in older English.
Some continental   squibs of Latin and Greek.
Nor did he forget   one of more recent renown
Gertrude she was called   first and last of the great modernists.
Did she ever write curiously   not unlike the old riddlers
that distant generation   become the ground of his world.
Laʒamon read those books.   He rifled their pages
lovely he found them   feathering them with his fingers
before turning to his notebooks   linking old lines together
riddling his reading   with runes of his own.

Slender Batons

Homage to Gertrude Stein

I.

Light blue and the same red with purple makes
A change. It shows that there is no mistake.

There can be breakages in Japanese.
A seal and matches and a swan and ivy.
It makes the shape and makes no melody.
The question does not come before there is

In any kind of place there is a top,
And the same red with purple makes a change,
A kind in glass, a spectacle and strange,
And more than any other if it is cheap.

A quite dark gray is monstrous ordinarily.
A lamp is not the only sign of glass.
A splendid address, a really splendid address
Cut cut in white, cut in white so lately.

II.

Aider, why aider why whow, whow stop.
Pick a ticket, pick it in strange steps.

Is there no rubbing, why is there no special,
And chew all bolts, and reckless, reckless rats
Within, within the cut and slender joints.
It showed that it was open, that is all.

Suppose it is within a gate which open
Is open at the closing hour of summer,
And bend more slender accents than have ever,
Than little women, really little women

Hurt and a red balloon and an under coat.
Not back again, back it was returned.
The least thing means a little flower and
No bill, no care, no past pearl pearl goat.

III.

A blend is that which holds no mice and this,
Which showed that was when there was no eclipse.

The regulation is that there is no
There is no doubt that to be right is more
No more disturbance than in little paper.
The stamp that is not only torn but also

The temperature, there is some use in it.
Put wetting where it will not do more harm.
A cape is not a cover in the summer.
And yet the time was not so difficult.

It did not hinder wood from not being used.
A little lingering lion and a chair.
The change, there comes the time to press more air,
So sullen and so low, so much refusal.

IV.

Act so that there is no use in a centre.
There is no wagon. There is no change lighter.

And it was so much smaller that a table.
Fitting a failing meant that any two.
Why is a pale white not paler than blue,
A silent star, a single spark, a little

And even if that has been lost there is
Is there a single piece of any color.
If the centre has the place then there
The whole, special suddenness commences

Blind and weak and organized and worried.
It shows the force of sacrifice and likeness.
A sack that has no opening suggests
A little movement and the bed is made.

The Ballad of Bender Sutton

Climb up a sight climb in the whole
  Cold coffee and a corn
A cup a stir and a behave
  All the goods are stolen

A ham is proud of cocoanut
  The hearts of onions aim
A bunch of likes that is to say
  It is not the same

A little leaf upon a scene
  An ocean any where
Utter needles and a guess
  It was a shame to stare

This makes it art and it is wet
  A check with stripes between
This makes a whole little hill
  Why is it so seen

In curled lash and little bits
  And mostly in remains
Is ex a cake suppose it is
  This means a solemn change

Alas the pull alas the bell
  Hurry up you flutter
Alas the little put in leaf
  Alas the wedding butter

It is a need it is a need
So strange and singular
A little fit sun sat in shed
A tiny spot and bare

A cross and an unequal scream
Make violet, violet when
A simple sample set of old
And not less noisy than

Yet all the one in that we see
Meant cake it was a sign
And easy easy excellent
Not nearly so behind

Climb up a sight climb in the whole
Cold coffee and a corn
A cup a stir and a behave
All the goods are stolen

Van Gogh Dropped

a ribbon on his meadow
dabbed of green and yellow
with one roof gash red
the last in the village
dividing storm darkened hills
from the sun bright meadow
on which he permitted
one blue streak to float
over the bloom filled field
making zephyr of error.

Van Gogh brushed
one dropped blue drop
back over blossoms
as boldly as Coyote
stared back at us
licking and sniffing
his maimed hind leg
a red bouquet of stump
going bad before loping
three legged into blue
woods filling with snow.

His Armory Show, Nights of 1958

Now it was beginning to seem he would not be an engineer
 Under the gallery lights he bent again to his books
  Drowsy as he slipped beneath the deepening weight of winter
   Erotic time he waded through as the clock hand crept ahead
    Draping itself it seemed in owlland's drift of snow
     Easy, yes, all too, to imagine Ann or Elaine down to her skin
      Security his assignment once they'd cut his scholarship
       C's in lit and language, D's in calculus and physics
        Exactly the formula to place a freshman on probation
         Never had he seen paintings such as these, as this
          "Describing an Inclined Plane" he might have called it
           Incompatible with the ordinary that slinky down the stairs
            Not that anything is ordinary once looked into
             Grinning, grinning, how the painter grasped his work
              A straight edge and a compass among his favorite tools
               Strange that key to compulsion within what's never clear
                That could be considered cheating not drawing freehand
                 As warmly yellow browns moved all to mold his eye
                  Inside for nightlong stretches the museum to himself
                   Rare wilderness this world of art and now some news of it
                    Could he calculate the curve of thought that launched that
                     Arc away from servitude to the useful and the needed
                      Such as exams he bent toward at this desk beneath Duchamp
                       Even while he dreamed of racing through his next rounds nude

After Claes Oldenburg

A small drawing, a
sketch in faded red,
Crusoe's umbrella,
the spark and, dropped,
its dissolution
in watercolor,
on its side, spanning
an island, heaped up
sand, a featureless
sea stranded under
a featureless sky,
as implied by wide
matting, and standing
for his enterprise—
that he'd reinvent
one most needed thing
(parasol, *para*
aqua), that nimble
fingers enabled
him to remember
how to stretch a piece
of sail out over
makeshift ribs and march
them back to back from
a center post like
dueling marksmen. What
flared for that, what feel
for particulars,
before he saw his
ship come in, and seeing
saw his fire go out?

Homage to Alfred Montgomery, Corn Painter

As winds rushed over the barn
a peck of corn tipped
to its side on the floor.

The empty basket made the barn
seem emptier
as beams of moony night
picked six ears of corn
out from the dark face
of the basket.

The wind over rafters
the hay loft bare
the mow door open
bats racing out and in.

The mow door bangs against the wall
and a few ears of corn
gleam like a silk skirt on the barn floor.

On the Last Days of Fast Time

October sun's a grave digger. These mornings
Tuck us back into the earth, heaving

Night above our highest sill. Instead
Of running under Orion's knife, as if
To fill the dipper with my frosted breath,
I return to yoga, stand on my head,

And bowing to the world's flow, I wait
For water to boil. Then I brew tea
And revise old poems. Summer's history,
But I'm not ready to seal the garden's fate

And turn it under. October revs the park
Oaks, each one one more weariness bronzed off,
Rooted but following careening earth
On her old headlong shuffle through the dark.

Neither Venice Nor Belmont

On such a night as this, on the bluff, around
The corner from the red brick Methodist and

Clapboard Baptist Churches, an abandoned
High school stands, "*Pro Populo*, 1904."
A pickup rests on blocks beside the door,
By which, from framing bas-relief medallions

Shakespeare and Jefferson look over bottomland,
Where oaks descend to willows beside a muddy
River. Behind them—soft!—a ghost prom party
Dances on a weathered floor, with a band,

With windows open, with women who remember cars
Along the levee, and summer nights like this—
Some garments loosed like silken wisps
Of cloud scraps overhead—when we were stars.

Fable

I've read how Odysseus, the well wandered, put an oar
upon his shoulder and walked inland until someone asked
why he carried a winnow fan. Then after the sacrifices,
he returned home, leaving his oar athwart a field boundary,
a witching rod for the first farm boy who saw no winnow fan.
I watched him as he learned by feel how it would lift grain
awkwardly, how by fingering the fulcrum's indecipherable
old mark, he found it knew no point of balance but took
steadying by hand, how, after drawing it across a fence,
he felt a moment of pull and caress, sweet hints of the sea
in deep pasture grass, as he drew the handle back a bit
before the blade struck ground. And I followed him
downland with it until he met men living who knew nothing
of close-grained wheat, or of fans made truly weighted
that skipped within the grain, that tossed seed heads,
chaff loosening, against a smoldering sun: men who mixed
their food with salt, strolled with women beside blue water,
with here and there an oar riding a willing shoulder.

Charlie Asked

whether I got morning sickness
that visceral storm
because he always did.
Not that I could remember
though that night I dreamed I lay in a new furrow
in the Middle Field
under one of its two lone basswood trees.
I lay in black earth rolled fresh
against the lime-lime green of new wheat in spring.
I lay bare as a baby
and folded like a knife
and pushed a child out onto the land

and felt the gravity of it
as if the day were
falling through me. I lay
more naked than when plowing
in December with snow flurries in the air, the
tractor's canvas sheath
funneling motor warmth into my face
before having to begin
my complaining crawl south, the north wind flaying
my backbone. So my dance from
one foot to the other
as the plow reopened the field's sweet skin.

Before the Jugs in Soaked Burlap, Before the Water

As boys we'd compete at chopping careless weeds,
at casting out our hoes and snapping them back
down cleanly through the base of rain-hogging stalks
that toppled at a stroke without our breaking
stride, except to sprawl beneath cottonwoods,
to drink from jugs wrapped in soaked burlap,
to imagine water seeping to the corn,
to watch Dad leaning on his hoe, scanning
the tree line—twenty acres he'd not clear,
twenty to remind us of hundreds that he had—
to watch him watch a redtail rising, rising.

Flagging for Alfatox in a Middle Field

The sun drops red behind the cottonwood
as my father makes his turn across the field

and aims around on the rag I stand waving.
In the distance, Dad's small, his tractor

silent on alfalfa as evening settles in.
Field sparrows, perching on ragged stems,

shake ripples out across the grain of wind.
We all tread space like the sun that lingers

on the swallows' flash as they skim
the alfalfa then loop up over a contrail

thinning, thinning. Then redwing defends
the drainage ditch with his bony, rattling call.

Softly falls the spray across the field,
caressing each alfalfa head, scattering

sparrows, weevil, and quail. The tractor
slowly swallows redwing's hot-winged cry.

Kindnesses

"You are very nice,"
a lady called from her car
        after watching me

    help Old Cat across
the street. But she hadn't seen
        my brother ditch his

    car to miss Rabbit
his first night out with a date,
        or our uncle pitch

    and swerve his pickup
to avoid a butterfly,
        or lift worms in cupped

    hands from a raw post
hole, or turn ants from Ground Hog's
        door as in he burst

    on Old Hog, touching
match to gas while saying, "I
        hope the folks are home."

Noctua

She wore a jacket with blouse buttoned high, a tie,
a bow, or a pin. She taught journalism and oversaw

our yearbook, the *Noctua*, which is Latin for night
bird or owl. She had graduated from a college

across the river, and her husband was a farmer.
She wore thin-rimmed glasses, her white hair up off

her shoulder. Her senior English class read one play
by Shakespeare, a few pages of Milton and Chaucer.

I never knew her given name and in our yearbooks
found only Mrs. Ambrose Wilson beside Marie,

Mrs. Mary, Byrdie Lee, and Ruth. What I remember
is *The Forsyte Saga*, nine hundred pages, one serious

charcoal volume. We were each issued our copy,
our assignment no whim of a year but Mrs. Wilson's

long practice: several chapters a day that we could
avoid reading if we would only listen to her retell

the adventures of Soames, that man of property,
of Irene, his wife, and her architect lover; of Irene's

second husband, a cousin of Soames; of Fleur, Soames'
beloved daughter, and handsome Jon, the son of Irene

and the cousin, and you can see where the owl probes.
What attracted her so, what made that block of a book

her medium for sending us into the world? I was attracted
to Dee Gensler, with dancing eyes, freckles, a quick laugh,

and a daughter, having run on ahead of my night thoughts
of nipples and silk. Alphabetical seating placed us together.

We whispered the plot and she said nothing of college.
And Mrs. Ambrose Wilson, about my age now, tall,

slender, and living with her husband, I haven't the least
idea of how much as his property, or what violations she,

like Irene, may have suffered. I only hear John Galsworthy
singing to her as she led us through his novel, as she

read alone on her farm porch through moist April and May
evenings. The lilacs sighing over choices many had made,

that Dee had made already, as may have Winged Night
with his tumor, who would come for her only ten years later.

Many Moons

The boy raced from
street lamp to street
lamp all the way
home and each time
his shadow flung
itself forward
to be pulled back
under foot un-
til lagging it
recovered to
catch him once more.

Marginalia Found in a Secondhand Catullus

Dubious passengers, all my old plunders

The summer night, the southwind too would listen

These things put an edge on the earth

Even the dune's ripples drop into stone

She was softer than paper under the heal of my hand

Swa-swa swallow slant's the sky's rhyme

Softer than snow on the garden falling

Wulf and Eadwacer

from the Old English

My people intend to toy with him.
They mean to corner him and murder him.
   How different with us.
Wulf waits on an island, I on another.
His island is alive with swamps,
With angry men roaming all over it.
They mean to corner Wulf and murder him.
   How different with us.

I've kept hope through Wulf's wanderings.
When I sat weeping, watching rain,
A stormy villager bound me to his arms.
He brought both joy and injury.
O Wulf, hoping for your rare visits
Has wasted my heart.
   It wasn't just hunger.

Do you hear, Eadwacer?
Wulf bears our whelp to the woods.
He scatters easily what we never gathered,
   Our way together.

From the Old English Riddles

The wind slings fresh flyers
off the mountainslopes.
Quick as night and just
as noisy, they coast crying,
from the wooded slopes,
to the timbered shores,
to the eaves even
of human children.

Swallows

A moth ate words.
What a wonderous thing
for a worm to swallow
the song of some man.
He devoured sentences,
all their substantiation.
But the shy scholar
was no whit the wiser
for swallowing words.

Bookworm

Like a silken shiver I slide
through my shelter. Whenever
I wish I turn against its demands.
It rolls right on over my resistance.
I prosper only within its premises.
But ya gotta love my leaping.

Fish in River

I watched a golden girl,
her hair cascading,
slip toward a dark garden
and its shadowy lanes,
and my intruding spirit
followed her farther,
that young friend of night.

Thoughts flew, waste
moistened the moment.
Day spun on indifferent
to whether she'd come
through it all right.

Sun following Moon

Bent over and pushing me out on the plain,
my master supports me and thrives, seeding my track.
All that I tear falls away.
I go sniffing the green to one side,
my clear trail clouding the other.
Anyone serving me well from behind
must have known his own master.

Plow

Beneath waves and the wind,
I breach cross-currents,
straining against
thatchworks of thought,
and find all homelands alien.
On stillness I depend,
lest hurled into flight,
my hands break from
their hold on the stones.

Anchor

CODA

All that I tear falls away—
sentences and their very foundation.

Dark and noisy night
beats against the eaves.

Mists rise. Dew moistens the earth.

All axioms prove alien.

Serranilla of Aranjuéz

One passenger crossing La Mancha
  wore the old worsted suit
he had worked in, black street shoes,
  intimate with fields,

and a sweatshirt the color of bone.
  I offered him a Camel,
because of our distance. "Sweet ones,"
  he said, "those and Luckies,"

before offering his own, less mellow.
  The single tooth in the front
of his mouth made him difficult to follow,
  that and the soft country

turns of his language. We reaped all
  the talk we could gather,
and worked it, from practical
  to carnival, about the *tierra*

we sped over. His tough cigarette
  was almost as good as his
smile; but his castanet
  wave when he left me at Aranjuéz—

muy debonaire, whatever his shoes said.

The Arab-Andalucian Lover and His Love

after Emilio García Gómez

I.

When you offer your cheeks, suffused with wine,
as the bearer cups to a libertine circle,
I do not reject the discipline.

For your color quickens all
who drink it in, as the grape
the pace of all who harvest vines.

II.

The day is fresh with dew
and the face of the earth
covered with the first
breath of flowers.

Your friend invites you
to two dishes steeped
in herbs and wine
on a secret hillside.

I would offer you more
were it not vulgar
to make much
of ones favors.

III.

"I send you a mirror so that your face
may rise in it." So wrote Ben al-Sabúni

and Don Emilio translated seven centuries
later and showed it to Lorca:

wine, fire, and laughter. "Thus knowing your
fairness, you'll forgive my lunatics."

More wine and more laughter as the cup dallied
around the full circle and Ben al-S.

bent to his verses. His next would beseach
all her benevolence. He smiled to think on it.

IV.

Remember your promise to visit the river?
Like the plum on your lips

sundown lingers on the water. Once more
our hearts could race the current

and your robe open like spring willow,
leading us to summer.

V.

Promises? Only
such as you shaped for
    yourself, as the wind
shapes the sand. How could
    I not seem to go
along with you? Why
    be surprised if I
slip through your fingers?

Ossabaw

small bones and shells
mud, silt and reinforcing grasses

something of salt
something of clear

the ground tugs at my feet

its medlay of marsh colors

     muhlenbergia

          that reddish pheasant

       plump in reedy juncus

the sweep of spartina
rills raveling sea lanes
a treeline traces inlet to river

the horizon sweeps wide

what but my heart
stirred learning

to respect the web

of the spider

a world opening to an opening eye

fritillaries

     flame orange

Nymphalidae

     skip off on swing

I learn to distribute my weight

under the first hints of swallows

their sums and long division
holding back to consider
sweeping in with corrections

before the salt wind

        old pedagogue

rings out his wet cloth
and wipes off the sky

grackles loud in the tree lanes
kingfisher counting
his stepping stone row
of old telephone poles

egrets tilt and haul in their sails

I come down the line each day
to watch heron stand

        straight and still

his attention to quicksilver pleasure

thoughts lost among filaments

a slight shift and he rows away

keeping vigil on

    the rolling underneath him

       spinning earth

small bones and shells

another lover of long views

a hawk on a limb

distinguishes a pine

sun beading water
fiddler crabs scribbling
their pockwork of holes

all trace and erasure

a painted bunting

shy harlequin

breath weight

low on the tree

Orion lifting high

           arching over

      the path of soft Pleiades

light on
      light green
and gold
       overlapping
fanwork
       dangling
an open
      necklace
twisting
     to slip
into grass

mud, stalk, silt

     and motion

three dorsal fins glide
through one turn

then a second
but abandon
their side stream
meander

      arch above their

             element

      in the bay's plaza

Pisces glimmers

        the twins step closer

               to the pole

a snake under long grass

    finding and filling a hole

the mouse drawn out

his clapper tail

        tip swinging

   wild and silent

        against the yielding air

dapple dawn Lancelot

            hovering

at rest

    the quick pump

of his tail

loving a sparrow's last

    wild release of self

their discovery of joint venture

     sparrow paints
     the wings of the raptor

leaves the air crystal

            qui qui qui qui qui qui

old clacker call

     cresserele

linked to flight

blue gash-galled

     burnished by coals

marsh grasses pitch
waves wash up river
vultures stagger
swallows and fritillaries
keep to their cover

intimacy

    into the mate

to love is to question

    coming closer

the feathers of kestrel
under the cedar
heron waiting
fails to grasp
the sweet flash
stirs the water

nudges desire

in sparing grows sparse

bending low

    ducking away from the web

a swarm of

    black birds

banks as one

    idea black

bird of

    scattered

parts

kestrel above them

    abandons her thought

        lets the wind sweep her

            smooth across marsh

grasses and water
shells compacting
between them

where the ground gives up

    something of salt

thoughts lost among filaments

    something of clear

swallows, fritillaries

the web of the spider . . .

Dust

My sweetheart marked the cross on my forehead
While she said those words. Kneeling, I glanced up

And we smiled. Never before had I given myself
To that ritual. My boyhood church thought it ostentatious.

For years I supposed it the stricken heart of Catholicism
Then learned to add others. If Paris was worth a mass,

What about a marriage? What could that be
But blossoming before her congregation?

The yellow stole of recent weeks exchanged
For lenten purple. Dust we are and shall be.

Dust I am have always been and so
Will I return. As wheat is vegetable matter

And so too all my flowers. No bloom however
Brilliant amounts to more than matter. The lofty

Oak reduces to sawdust, pulp, or ash.
Our bag of mostly water shrivels, dries up.

No light, electric pulse, or intelligence is ours.
All otherness is His, although we don't

Like putting it that way either anymore.
Easter was ever festive. The altar golden,

White and flowered. Greenery around each
Pillar curving all around the nave. Flowers

Woven into green, and a cage at every
Pillar top. Canaries, white and yellow,

Singing, singing, with our pastor and the choir.
A gentle effervescence that I perched above.

How did I resist? All lent I'd feel all but
Pushed off that balcony onto the central aisle

To accept my Lord and Savior. The tiny clink
Of communion glasses rustled in the pews, but I

Never volunteered, never took the wine or bread,
Denied the stone bath in the corner, could not

Believe in Father, Lord, Redeeming Son,
Life Everlasting, dust reformed and shining,

Refused to offer up my spark—if not
Just dust—and who was watching anyway

This speck of matter lost in galactic space,
Home to mass extinctions every few hundred

Million years, the Pleistocene, or age of humans,
Not even era-worthy in a string of -zoics,

Ceno- and four more, through which string spores,
Mosses, ferns, and conifers, ginkgoes before grasses,

And all before our kind, the drift of continents
Do-si-do-ing over vasty oceans,

Curling back into each other and spinning out
Again, volcanoes and meteors ushering ages out

And in, through doors beyond disaster through which
Dung beetles have survived. Who'd dream up

A Father inspired enough to call that dance?
Besides, if other corners of creation offered

No more to watch than we, 'twas one poor universe,
Or only fakey vast, though we had offered up

To grisly end one wild radiant Woodstock
Rabbi angel radical who sings to us assuming, us-

Ness in this tiny torch of matter, one brow of which
I lifted to her touch as to canaries caged and singing.

The Blue He Seized

after Antonello da Messina's "Annunciation" (c. 1475)

Perhaps she heard a child cry, her niece or daughter.
Perhaps Antonello spoke from behind her
while cleaning his brush. A blue shawl
frames his virgin's face, dividing her from midnight.
Flaws in the background could be read as stars.
Her left hand pulls the shawl to her breast.
Her right rises from an open book, fingers
miming her surprise.

                Perhaps he offered
a glass of red wine and a section of orange.
Perhaps his fingers, sticky with orange,
will graze her lips before checking her place
in the prophets as he remembers temples
high over the sea and an ancient theater
where air was nectar for shepherds, and long views
implied all Greek abstraction. To the side lay fields,
tilled longer than the temples knew—"the oldest
of gods, the earth, immortal, we wear away,
our plows, year in, year out"—so an old chorus.
And beyond the fields, the sea.

                  There's the blue
Antonello seized for the shawl and eyes
of his literate virgin. For the sea extends
beyond horizons, never drawing a line,
and therefore less innocent, fading as a red
dress fades into a woman's cheek as scripture
settles into her knowing, as poppies fade
from crimson in Tuscany to orange below Rome,
to Sicilian starlight awakening Mary.

Looking for Mother

Two women sit on a porch,
the one in a rocker leans forward

toward the other,
Grandmother,

who sits listening, head lowered.
A small tree sweeps upward

behind her shoulder, or two
trees, or is it one

divided, a birch?
Its lower branches

loom over a railing, like the head
of a moose down the road.

How often did you sit for these
snapshots from the twenties,

in quick strokes, in charcoal?
He taught art in the schools.

His father painted houses,
was he an avant garde house painter

telling clients after a few broad sweeps
across a wall, "I'm leaving

the rest to you, you must become
co-creator of our work,"

art being "what you can get away
with" as Grandfather knew but likely

had not heard, though who
knows the murmurs of the Art Institute

of his youth in excited Chicago?
This sketch, or study, how

important to Grandfather?
What was he saying of Grandmother,

once again conscripted?
In the foreground to her side,

a girl leans back in her rocker,
her head in the comics,

ignoring her elders and so stealing the scene.
She might be thirteen,

a year, at most two,
from the death of her father, of whom

I have but this sketch: architecture
abandoned, tennis and chess,

second hand book stores—a thousand
volumes sold

soon at a dime
each, dozens

of boxes but no money,
not to speak of. How he

studies his daughter,
one dark dot

her eye, her right knee cocked away from
her left—"Should I be one of them?"—

she asks, turning to pick
up a *National Geographic.*

Ciao

The branch has its faithful birds
because it does not bind, it offers.
— Pedro Salinas

The branch is faithful to the birds, extending
a greeting.

The tree is faithful to the branch, supportive of all
its ramification.

The earth is faithful to the tree, embracing
source beyond seeing.

The sky is faithful to the earth though parched
and distracted

by birds who scatter its best thoughts, its deep
blue thinking.

Half Music, Half Murmur

Weeds, redeeming weeds, and vines returning brown.
Crisped edges tangle on the matted ground.
Potatoes brush against my spade, potatoes brown.

Canes, long-leaning canes, their rigor weighted down.
Raspberries cluster close above the ground,
Berries steeped in summer, intensely dangling down,

Against the scarab grackles, brilliant then gone.

Popular Song for a Popular Season

This color's getting out
of hand. Even today as
the first snowy thought

coarsens October
the park oaks careen
flamboyant. Runners cruise

more winded down the slopes
as fire blasts all breath out
overhead. A long draft

sucks the swimming pool dry.
Sumacs quiver on
dactylous embers.

Still the sky restrains its
wet blanket; each vagrant
flame steps out on its limb.

Twenty Ways To Say Snow

Glints on the dog's back
Breaks up like shale
Dissolves on contact
Pelts us like hail

Damasks the highway
Lines lashes with glue
Lures out the sleigh
Corns stalks show through

Step lightly on top of
Makes power lines sag
Sticks to the shovel
Melts grocery bags

Keeps track of the fox
Slows Owl's wings
A hedgerow in socks
Gowned cedars sing

Holds Moon to the solstice
Shows hope uncongealed
Don't spin or it's ice
It beds down the field

Serranilla of Barranquilla

after "Serranilla de la Finojosa," Marqúes de Santillana (1398–1458)

No barmaid so well assayed
Had I found in poesia,
As Blanda, the sadly arrayed
Sweetheart of Barranquilla.

Finding my way
From college to after
In a city betrayed
Along the edge of its laughter,
She was melopoeia,
A song's lovely burden,
Though surely no virgen,
Not Blanda of Barranquilla.

In a shaded courtyard
Set out with small tables,
And doors leading darkward
As a few bucks enabled,
We were the cavalleria
And she our trainer,
Long night the retainer
Of Blanda of Barranquilla.

It could be that first roses
May have been so composed

And as fresh in their poses
Saying all I suppose
Had they sung Ave Maria
As in crinolines faded,
With a few drinks aided,
Blanda danced Barranquilla.

I tried not to stare
At her beauty surprising,
Being somewhat aware
Of sentiments rising,
But as if offering spiraea
I ventured before her,
And as if I adored her
Asked of Blanda of Barranquilla.

And then with a smile,
"Welcome stranger," she replied,
"I understand well
Just what you've implied.
But she has no idea
Of love and knows where
You're drifting—nowhere
Near Blanda of Barranquilla."

Like Smoke

Like smoke from pistols starting distant races
Or fleeting whitecaps far beyond the sandbar
Or galaxies on headlong outward courses

Faintly suspected by the hushed astronomer
Like gestures seen developing in the basin
    Of smoke from pistols starting distant races
    Or fleeting whitecaps far beyond the sandbar

Before the fixative freezes another picture
Of an image that could almost glisten
Another gesture fading on the horizon
    Like smoke from pistols starting distant races
    Or galaxies on headlong outward courses
    Or fleeting whitecaps far beyond the sandbar

Beige and Avocado

for Luther Dickerson

After years and years
I've returned to the grave
of a sophomore
friend barely able

to remember what
he was—an uncertain
squareness of the shoulders,
a flair for draftsmanship,

a shufflestep
dogging his jumpshot.
Then one October night,
avoiding his father,

after an incident
with his employer,
he put a bullet in his head.
I think his eyes were blue.

I remember best
our own exposure,
his best friend lost
in grief, my swift knowledge

of sudden promotion,
his girlfriend crying
all day long
in the auditorium,

our excursions all week
to the open casket,
the lump as native
to the side of his head

as the postures we
were learning, staring
death in the face,
forming condolences,

then bearing with friends
a friend to his grave,
our lives lifted to story.
Luther, I took Cathy

to our prom and learned
from her gown two
new words for color,
here in these flowers

I've found for you,
beneath a small stone,
along the margins
of my boyhood.

What You Can Get Away With

Once it was a fur-lined room like a muff
made of clippings swept up off barbers' floors;

then there was the two-by-four with three sixteen-
penny nails hammered halfway in and strings tied

to each and drawn to a nail beneath bright light
high on the wall. As your eye followed string

it found pencil-drawn lines tied to a pencil-drawn nail.
Then the gallery I couldn't even enter as lights

from within cast back my shadow. As I stopped
with one foot raised over hundreds of thumbtacks,

thousands of thumbtacks, heads down, tacks up,
in perfect, shiny rows like a tiny field of brassy,

Iowa corn. It was a summer evening, and I wore
flipflops. In those days I wore flipflops all over,

mile after mile. There was no between to those rows.
Just tacks shoulder to shoulder all across the room.

I could have set my foot against heads of rows
and swept away a space where I might stand. But I

was an attendant lord, soon down on my knees, extending
an arm and hand. I brought my palm down carefully,

barely touching tacks, and wiggled them to see what
had been risked avoiding glue. Other viewers leaned

over me. I touched an ear to floor, let my eyes run out
over tips of tacks and watched the play of shadow define

row after row before rising to find photographs
of "throwing one's voice": a new-born caged with a macaw,

a macaw trained by the parent; then a warehouse in Venice:
cinders, rock, and hundreds of open jars, paired lip

to lip, as art waits for one to fall, whenever the earth moves,
listens for the tremors of distant shattering glass.

Too Trillium

Old leaves, sticks, and brown
cedar fingers lie strewn
in your angle of stone.

Each May I await
your quiet return.
You give no early hints

before your broad
green spades spill out.
From your tuberous

and moist native place
you carve a hole in air
and justify the neighborhood.

Not even flies disturb
your stillness as the cavern
around you collapses

on ivory petals over-
lapping on creped edges
and you slide into

your better season:
your blooms browned
and wilting, drifting

beyond the bluster of roses—
just shades of June shadows,
your arid traces.

Oriole

I can take you to him, if you can spare the hour. Yellowthroat too
and goldfinches in bunches. The brown thrasher, shy improviser,
and the breast-spotted song sparrow. They've always been around,
like stamps from tropical republics, so I must be learning to look.
So much so close to us remains unseen. To look and to listen for first
I hear their songs. Not that I could describe his except to say sharper
than finches, with several clear notes ending, and different from
the cardinal that you too by now may have come to know. I'd been
scanning the sky for raptors then began to notice the leafy woods
and underbrush. I'd be walking along watching Ramón sniff one
long, grassy clump after another, hear a song and remember, like
recalling an island to which I'd longed to travel, that's oriole.
I suppose the New World cardinal was named for the Old, not
the other way around. But the oriole, to find him flashing is like
stealing in a silent canoe to a lush and silent shore.

Blinded

I glimpsed a dove, then a second through our bedroom skylight. High in the cedar between our house and our neighbor's in scraggly limbs where I rarely think to look. Dove brown with subtle spots on tail feathers that wink in streams of early morning light. I cannot follow the arc of their flights though I sometimes catch them fluttering from one limb to another. They may have their nest nearby, just beyond our range of sight. Soon I'll go out and buy our Sunday paper. I don't even know the color of their eggs, though I've heard their cooing all my life.

Papaver

This spring poppies surprised us. I seeded them last summer but forgot where. Blossoms that had gladdened all of Italy and that, seeing once, I'd been unable to forget, flowered at home. Some old soldiers had known how to collect the seeds as I had not. I'd bought a dollar packet from an Amish gardener. Now I know what to look for after the blossoms fade though closer attention to bagels might have taught me that. Before they flooded us with a month of sunrise, I had almost weeded them out. The hand of grace alone had stayed me. Now I've turned more soil over and raked it fine to help them spread. I didn't miss all those eons that came before me, nor will I those that roll through next. One motive for turning up next spring is to see how far these poppies spread. Watching them today made me think of that, that and your smile as you stood with me.

From a Journal

I.

Throughout the Village by night, hummingbirds
take wing, wings of the most lightly vertebrate:
after the car passes, the painter, from shadows, pounces
on a back fence or a window box—stencils, sprays,
and an arts grant, catalog, and map for a walking tour.
I found the evidence in the Strand but soon gave
the book away, saving the idea for later, in Iowa City.

II.

Like one red pictogram amid calligraphy
like one heart unfrozen, quickening your own,
like the apt word on your lips when you thought
to say exactly what you exactly thought:
the high cardinal singing, you note it now,
on his tree, no leaf, snow loads the ground;
like one coal in the grate and from somewhere
breath enough to blow it into spring.

III.

I'm learning to listen to my espresso maker fill,
to hear, not watch, water lip up to the blow hole,
because I thought it could prove possible,
I might employ the idle of another kitchen moment,
because the light is dimming, the fine lines fade,
because the light is dimming and I imagined angels
leaning in to listen as if it were a riddle, all
my fine discriminations, in the shade of asphodel.

IV.

Yesterday the goldfinches returned
to the thistle feeder. They'd ignored it all winter
but now, as the first smudge of gold shows in their coats
they light in the birch and test thistle gone stale.
Ramón lolls underneath on melting crusts of snow.
I'm behind an upstairs window, wavering on one
leg, doing "tree," trying to forget looking on.

The Secret Lives of Trees

She's much too much,
that dogwood, lifting
her slip on lightly
wooded hillsides
then finding her cheeks
multitudes of cheeks
come scarlet, come fall.

Only our pronouns
compromise her.
She may not be she
at all. Or
the attenuation
of her early blossom
conveys another

story. Pale,
they are,
mausoleum
pale, curling
from dulled purple
centers, preparing
to drift like grandmothers
from wicker rockers
on long porches.

And the leaves, the late
scarlet leaves,
are an old woman's memories,
turning to touch
the patriarch oak to fire.

Foucault Would Have Said

My father and I worked the Long Narrow Field.
We had sharpened our hoes with a heavy file.

I preferred a thin-bladed hoe to one shaped
like a slice of bread. The file put a gleam

on its edge that I could whip down through head
high stalks of pigweed or clumps of volunteer

corn, seeded from what had fallen the year before.
We worked half mile rows with groves of cottonwood,

mulberry, box elder, willow, and plum marking
each end of the field. A glass jug of well water

wrapped in soaked gunnysack lay stashed in shade
near the road. How fine it was to look back out over

our labor and see a new crop unmarred by weeds
or wild corn. We made clear what kind of farmers

we were, as if in a suburban competition of lawn.
"Maybe you should consider a good college,

Harvard or Yale, someplace like that." Father
sliced through thick careless weed just then

though I remembered how he had admonished
me for getting down from my tractor to walk

out to the road to speak to a man who hadn't
even stepped in his city shoes from his city car.

I knew the names from lists of scores in the *Star*.
Amherst, Bates, Bowdoin, all the way to UCLA

and Washington State. So I signed up to meet
"a representative of a New England mens' college"

in January, by which time I had forgotten. A note
came around to fetch me from class. Dee winked

encouragement, and I joined a few friends to listen
to a man who didn't even name his college the first

half hour. When I sat with Dee again the next day,
I doubt that I mentioned my application papers.

After Maillol

The more motionless young girls
are, the more they seem to move.

When sculpture isn't good,
it is hard under your hand.

Bound Each to Each

Our hearts leapt up as we beheld it. "Did
You see the rainbow?" "I did, I did," we said,

Up and down philosophical halls and always
With a smile, as if we'd won permission,
Our lonely projects stunned into remission
By rapture under heaven's occult ways.

Yellow over green, a narrow lawn
Beside a sandy path. But the lavender,
"A pale to light purple to light or paler
Violet." To either side, new spectra dawn,

Diminish, and fade into degrees of blue.
Within one, a hint of orange, just a thread.
At last, one least violence, now red,
A touch of red, before violet's blue rescue.

Anasazi Baskets

The ancients wove these baskets to hold water.
Shoots springing subtle from beneath the soil,
How they tugged on willow threads

That rose *sub-tela*, as Romans said. "The smylere
With the knyf under the cloke," Borges thought—
    Our ancients wove these baskets to hold water,
    Shoots springing subtle from beneath the soil—

The line of romance that foresaw the novel,
"Densely woven," an Anasazi gloss
Upon "a subtil gerland for hire hede"
    Since ancients wove these baskets to hold water,
    Shoots springing subtle from beneath the soil.
    How they snugged their willow threads.

On Never Ending with . . .

An ax works mostly by its own sufficient
Force, on your aim much more dependent

Than on your arm. Select a grain in a log,
Place two blows as if they were twin brothers,
And without more work, most open for the fire.
But willow sprouts in fields prove pedagogues

More difficult. You must learn to strike
Beneath the soil, where earth, rewoven all
Winter, supports the subtle shoot. How genial
Then your knowing cut, exactly quick

And gleaming like the air your axe glides through.
But hit it high, not that unusual,
And the willow stings inside your hand, then all
The way, your arm and eye, back out up in to.

Poison, a partially found poem

"The Romans had a word for it, 'gravitas,'
a core, a weight of judgment and honest
appraisal"—so, gravely, the commencement
speaker, schooled on Cicero and Virgil,
a graduate of Amherst and Harvard
who had counseled Japanese internment
during the nineteen forties and applied
"benign obstruction" during those same years
toward the rescue of European Jews.
He blocked their refugee admission
to the United States for reasons
of "Army morale"; then, summoned again
to Washington in the middle sixties,
knew, by his gravitas a "crucial test" when
he saw one and said, "You've got to go in."

An American Suite

Found Poems from the Journals of Lewis and Clark

In a northerly direction from the mouth of the creek
in a plain is a hill that by different Indians
from all over this quarter is supposed the residence
of deavels. They are human in form with remarkable
large heads, about a foot and a half high, very watchful,
and armed with sharp arrows. Tradition informs
that many have suffered by these little people.
Three Mahars fell to their fury not many
years sence. The surrounding plain is void
of timber and leavel to a great extent.
The wind from whatever quarter it blows
drives over the plains and against it. Insects
are driven to its leeward side, and small birds
resort to this place in surch of them, particularly
the small brown martin. From the top of this mound
we beheld a most butifull landscape. Buffalow
were seen, feeding in various directions.
The plain rising far to the north, n.w. & n.e.
extends without interruption. We set the prairies
on fire to signal to the Soues to come to the river.

— AUGUST 1804

In the evening the men discovered a large brown bear
and six good hunters went out to attack him.
Two reserved their fires as had been conscerted.
The four others fired nearly together and each
put his bullet through him. Two of the balls
passed through the bulk of both lobes of his lungs.
In an instant the monster ran at them, his mouth
wide open. The two who had reserved their fires
discharged their pieces. Boath of them struck him,
one only slightly, the other broke his shoulder,
retarding his motion a moment. The men, unable
to reload, took flight. Two betook themselves
to a canoe; the others ran into willows
and reloaded their pieces. Each discharged his,
but the guns served only to direct the bear.
Two he pursued so close that they were obliged
to throw their guns aside and themselves into the river.
So enraged was this anamal that he plunged
only a few feet behind the second compelled
to the water, when a man on shore shot him
through the head and killed him. Eight balls
had passed through him in different directions.
The bear being old the flesh was indifferent.
They only took the skin and the fleece.
The latter made us several gallons of oil.

—MAY 1805

The persons who visit the entrance of this river
for the purpose of hunting or traffic are either
American or English. The Indians inform us
they speak the same language and give proof
by their words of English, as musquit, powder,
shot, damned rascal, sun of a bitch, &c.

—JANUARY 1806

For Coyote, Song and Lament

Old Man Coyote lost his skin.
  We are going to tan it.
We'll scrape the meat right off it.
  We'll salt and scrape and wash it.

Old Man Coyote's grown more thin.
  We've soaked his hide in alum,
In salt and washing soda, sunk
  His snout in sudsy water.

Old Man Coyote packs it in.
  He can't inspire the prairie.
He's flat upon a plank now,
  His shadow cannot find him.

Coyote left it on the grass,
  Running 'cross the meadow.
We spread it on our workbench,
  Hold what held his nature in.

The Collector

My letter had raised a question
so he asked a few more, what had taken

me there right after college
what had I hoped to find, why did I wish to change

course & those few were not answered all at
once nor are they likely to be exact

though their tenor is true
enough, I sought admission to graduate school

with an M.A. I might move from Barranquilla
to Rio, Italy, India

or France, there were schools
all over & many taught English, I was two

years out almost, a homeroom teacher
of fourth & fifth graders

& had thought to write Columbia
(with a "u") where a few pals had gone & Virginia

on the word of my wife's most recent roommate
& nowhere else for I knew little of graduate

schools, so my letter
to Professor Fredson Bowers

for whom a general was just then
being named in *Frankenstein*

Meets the Space Monster "about an astronaut
transformed into Frankenstein while visiting a dying planet"

which was of course earth & whom I would soon
overhear pooh-poohing

the recommendations that he had been
cornered to write to win

grants for fledgling professors, who needs grants
he would ask, they haven't the guts

to be scholars
a good scholar

is like a poet you can't stop him
& of course he said "him"

as we all did & our
correspondence flourished for

something about my letters he found attractive
perhaps the oddity of my having

got to Barranquilla or perhaps
my reflections on the *Alianza para Progresso*

one of our new president's pet
projects or what it felt

like to have hunched down
across the Caribbean

south of Havana
my ear to the short wave

radio during the Missile Crisis
numbering the probable uses

for an English teacher
had things gone differently that October

with luck I could be the boy
in the bar shining shoes

until at last I held
his decision in hand

my grades were not
what he sought

& I was stuck
where I could not take

certain exams they required
but I had endured

a worthy college so perhaps
I should give grad school a try, perhaps

he could find a gradership for me
far be it from him to leave me

stranded, having harvested more than he'd hoped
of my exceedingly colorful Colombian stamps.

Haiku Composed During a Lecture

The long needle pines
eloquent in the windows
    behind our speaker.

A snowbound robin
by the college library.
    How lost can he be?

Less the cardinal's
calligraphy, these haiku,
    than sparrows flyting.

Empty the bird bath,
empty the feeder, empty
    the snow fence, the snow.

One Sunday, he left
his car at the airport door,
    its engine running.

Notes

"Go, Little Book" derives, obliquely, from several riddles in Old English.

"Poem Ending with Lines from an Obscure Memoir" draws on that of my uncle, Henry W. Hamilton (1898–1984).

"After Laȝamon" is modeled on an introductory passage in Laȝamon's *Brut*.

The phrasing of all "Slender Batons" and the related ballad was found in Gertrude Stein.

"Van Gogh Dropped" refers to "Les Vessenots en Auvers," 1890, in Museo Thyssen-Bornemisza, Madrid.

Alfred Montgomery (1857–1922) was best known for his Midwestern still lifes and cornucopias: bushels and sacks and pecks of corn, often spilling over.

"Fable" plays off a passage toward the end of the *Odyssey* and echoes, in a few of its lines, the translation of Richmond Lattimore.

The poems of the Arab-Andalucian lover, but not the reply of his love, are translations, sometimes partial, of poems in Emilio García Gómez's *Poemas Arabigoandaluces*.

Ossabaw Island was once the home of a colony for artists and writers. My thanks to Eleanor West and her staff, especially C.B. and Al, for fruitful time there.

In "The Blue He Seized," the old chorus is from *Antigone* as translated by Robert Fagles. Antonello's "Annunciation" is in the Palazzo Abatellis in Palermo.

The Middle English passages in "Anasazi Baskets" are from Chaucer's "Knight's Tale."

The coyote and his shadow owe much to *Indian Tales*, by Jaime de Angulo, and a touch also to *King Lear*.

As I owe much to aiders and abettors over the years: Marvin Bell, Stavros Deligiorgis, Kathleen Flenniken, William Ford, John Kinsella, and James McKean.

www.ingramcontent.com/pod-product-compliance
Lightning Source LLC
Chambersburg PA
CBHW022034090426
42741CB00007B/1058